Table of Contents

4 CD Track Listing

Track 1: Tuning to a Piano
Track 2: Tuning to a Fiddle
Track 3: Fine Tuning the Strings
Track 4: Half Notes on the Open A String
Track 5: Half Notes and Quarter Notes on the Open A String
Track 6: Half Notes, Quarter Notes, and Eighth Notes on the Open A String
Track 7: Notes on the A String
Track 8: Hot Cross Buns, demonstration
Track 9: Hot Cross Buns, backing track
Track 10: Run Pony, Stop Pony rhythm
Track 11: Boil The Cabbage, demonstration
Track 12: Boil The Cabbage, backing track
Track 13: Switching Between the Open A and E Strings
Track 14: Notes on the E String
Track 15: Twinkle, Twinkle (basic version), demonstration
Track 16: Twinkle, Twinkle (basic version), backing track
Track 17: Chugga, Chugga, Stop, Stop rhythm
Track 18: Twinkle, Twinkle (Chugga Chugga version)
Track 19: Twinkle, Twinkle (Chugga Chugga version), backing track
Track 20: Dotted Exercise #1
Track 21: Dotted Exercise #2
Track 22: Dotted Exercise #3
Track 23: Dotted Exercise #4
Track 24: Liza Jane, demonstration
Track 25: Liza Jane, backing track
Track 26: Notes on the D String
Track 27: Notes on the D String Exercise
Track 28: Sixteenth notes on the D string
Track 29: D Major Scale Exercise
Track 30: Oh, Susanna, demonstration
Track 31: Oh, Susanna, backing track
Track 32: Notes on the G String
Track 33: Notes on the G String Exercise
Track 34: G Major Scale in Quarter Notes
Track 35: G Major Scale in Eighth Notes
Track 36: G Major Scale in Sixteenth Notes
Track 37: Dem Golden Slippers, demonstration
Track 38: Dem Golden Slippers, backing track
Track 39: Kickoff in A
Track 40: Kickoff in D
Track 41: Tag Ending in A #1
Track 42: Tag Ending in A #2
Track 43: Tag Ending in A #3
Track 44: Tag Ending in A #4
Track 45: Tag Ending in D #1
Track 46: Tag Ending in D #2
Track 47: Tag Ending in D #3
Track 48: Tag Ending in D #4
Track 49: Devil's Dream, demonstration
Track 50: Devil's Dream, backing track
Track 51: Old Joe Clark, demonstration
Track 52: Old Joe Clark, backing track
Track 53: Camptown Races, demonstration
Track 54: Camptown Races, backing track
Track 55: Cripple Creek, demonstration
Track 56: Cripple Creek, backing track

Welcome to *Absolute Beginners Fiddle!*

This book will teach you all of the essential basics you need to know to play the fiddle, from the very first time you take your fiddle out of its case, to playing your first songs.

The **easy-to-follow instructions** will guide you through:
Learning the parts of your fiddle
Care and maintenance of your fiddle
Changing strings
Tuning
Correct posture and playing position
Reading basic music notation, learning note names and understanding rhythm
Fingering and bowing techniques
Playing your first songs

Listen to the CD as you learn—the specially recorded audio will let you hear how the music should sound—then try playing the exercises and pieces along with the backing tracks.

And always remember: practice makes perfect! Practice regularly and often. It's better to practice for twenty minutes every day than once on the weekend with nothing in between.

The Fiddle

The Fiddle or the Violin?

There is no technical difference between the fiddle and the violin—they are the same instrument. Whether one refers to the instrument as a fiddle or violin depends on the way the instrument is played and the type of music played on the instrument.

When used to play the American folk music styles (such as bluegrass and old-time), the violin is referred to as a *fiddle*, and is played by a fiddler. A *violin* most often describes the instrument when it is used to play classical music, as performed by a violinist.

Also, some fiddlers will alter their instruments to accommodate the frequent *double stops* (two strings played at once) that are played in bluegrass fiddle music.

Parts of the Fiddle

- The *scroll* is located at the top of the fiddle and is often decorative.
- The *tuning pegs* are used to adjust the tuning of the fiddle by tightening or loosening the strings, and are inserted into the *peg box*.
- The fiddle has four *strings*: G, D, A, and E.
- The *fingerboard* runs down the length of the *neck* and is where the player presses the strings down to play notes.
- The *f-holes* (so-called because they are shaped like the cursive letter "f") allow for more sound to resonate from the instrument.
- The *bridge* is held in place by and supports the tension of the strings stretched over the body of the fiddle and transmits the vibrations of the strings throughout the body of the instrument.
- The *soundpost* is located under the bridge inside the fiddle, and supports the body of the instrument and helps to amplify the sound of the instrument.
- The *fine tuners* are used for making subtle adjustments to the tuning that do not require the loosening or tightening of the string at the tuning peg.
- The *tailpiece* and *nut* hold and support the strings across the length of the instrument.
- The *chin rest* helps the fiddler keep the instrument in place under the chin, keeping the fingering (left) hand free from having to support the instrument.

Taking Care of Your Fiddle

Fiddles are fragile, so be sure to take good care of your instrument:
1. Don't bump the fiddle into anything or drop it at any time.
2. Try not to expose the instrument to extreme heat or cold. At the very least, the strings will pop out of tune.
3. Make sure to wipe off the body of the fiddle and the fiddle strings after every time you play.

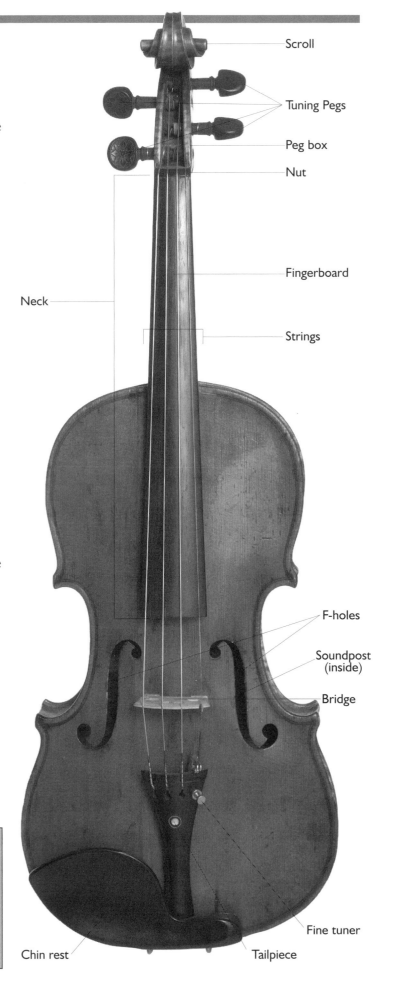

Scroll

Tuning Pegs

Peg box

Nut

Fingerboard

Neck

Strings

F-holes

Soundpost (inside)

Bridge

Fine tuner

Chin rest

Tailpiece

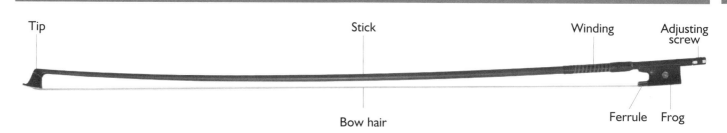

Tip Stick Winding Adjusting screw

Bow hair Ferrule Frog

The *bow* has horsehair stretched across the length of the *stick* which, when tightened, allows you to draw the bow across the strings to produce sound. Turn the *adjusting screw* at the end of the *frog* in a counterclockwise direction to tighten the bow hair.

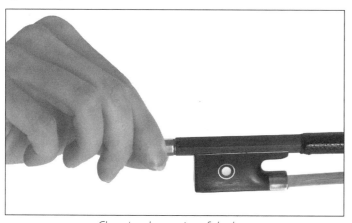

Changing the tension of the bow

The tension of the bow should be tight enough so that your pinky finger can almost fit through the middle of the bow.

Correct tension of tightened bow

Loosened bow

Do not over-tighten the bow! If the stick begins to curve in toward the hair of the bow, it is too tight and you should loosen it immediately. Over-tightening can warp the stick and ruin the bow.

Before returning the fiddle to its case, loosen the bow by turning the screw counterclockwise until the bow hair is flat against the stick. Loosening the bow tension when not playing will prevent the bow from warping.

TIP
When should you rosin your bow? When the bow starts to get a bit slick and no longer grips the strings, forcing you to push harder to produce a tone.

Rosining the Bow

Rosin is made from a variety of tree resins (mainly pine and other conifers) that are cooked and molded into the typical amber-colored box or cake form that you will find in your local music store.

When applied to the hair of the fiddle bow, rosin will enhance the sound production of the instrument by creating friction between the hair and the strings.

When using the fiddle for the first time, rosin the bow well. You may find that even after you have applied rosin to the bow, it still does not produce any sound on the strings. If this happens, rosin the bow again until it can get a proper grip on the strings. Re-apply rosin as needed (generally every few days), but sparingly.

Remember to wipe off the body of the fiddle and the fiddle strings with a soft cloth after you play. Otherwise, rosin will build up over time on the strings and fiddle and could damage your instrument.

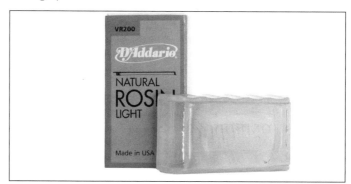

Rosin

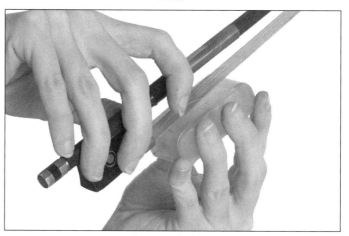

Rosining the bow

Strings

The variety of strings can be overwhelming at first. Strings are made from different types of materials—from the traditional gut-core to the modern synthetic- and steel-core—and are available in a wide range of brands and prices. There is no one kind of string that is best-suited for everyone. You want to find a string that complements the style of music you are playing, which may require some experimentation on your part.

A steel string with a medium string gauge (the diameter of the string) is best; the string will be a little harder to press down at first, but it produces a better volume and tone quality and tends to have a faster response. Steel strings are also less likely to react to changes in temperature and humidity and will tend to stay in tune longer than gut or synthetic strings. Steel strings can be purchased in complete sets of G, D, A, and E.

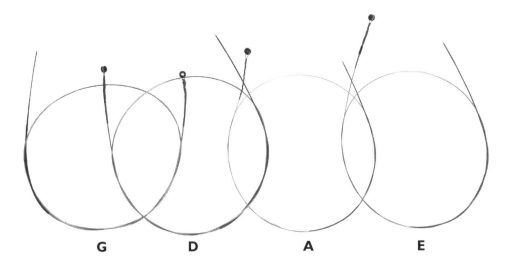

G   D   A   E

The Shoulder Rest

Shoulder rest

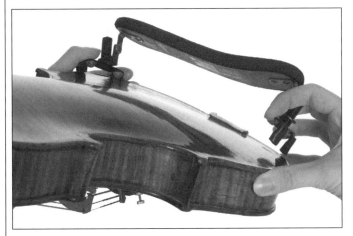

Putting on the shoulder rest

The kind of shoulder rest you select will depend on your size and build. When positioned correctly, the shoulder rest will help you to hold the fiddle between your chin and left shoulder so that your fingering (left) hand can remain free from supporting the neck of the fiddle to play the notes. You don't want your left wrist to rest on the fiddle at any time.

Correct left-hand wrist position

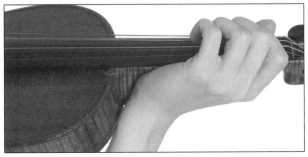

Incorrect left-hand wrist position

Playing Position

Stand up straight, facing forward with your feet placed shoulder-width apart.

Bring the fiddle up to rest on your left collarbone, holding it in a position parallel to the floor and slightly to the left side of your body.

With the fiddle resting comfortably on your collarbone, place your left-side jawline on the chin rest. In this position, you should be able to hold the instrument between your shoulder and chin without the support of your left arm, which you will need for fingering.

Fiddle positioned correctly on left shoulder

Holding the Fiddle

Placement of the Left Hand

To practice this, drop your left (or fiddle) arm to rest at your side. Then bring your left arm in a gentle curve back up to the instrument. Place your thumb on the neck of the fiddle opposite the first and second finger, not clutching onto the neck of the instrument but maintaining a relaxed curvature of the hand.

Remember to keep your wrist in a relaxed position, and avoid resting the wrist against the neck.

Repeat this exercise until moving your left hand from rest position to playing position becomes comfortable.

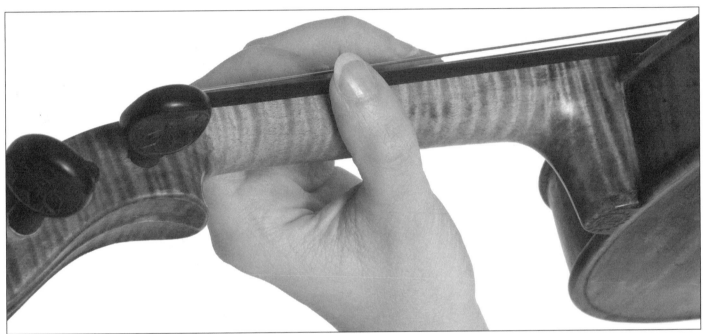

Correct position of left-hand thumb on neck

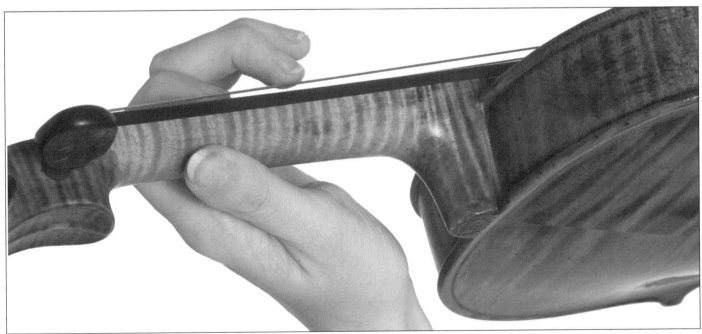

Incorrect: thumb placed under neck

Bow Grip

Bowing is by far the most challenging aspect of playing the fiddle. How you hold the bow, also known as your *bow grip*, will affect the sound production of your instrument, and getting a good, clean tone takes a lot of practice and patience.

The correct placement of your thumb is inside the frog.

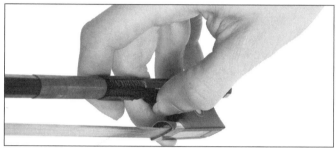

Correct placement of thumb

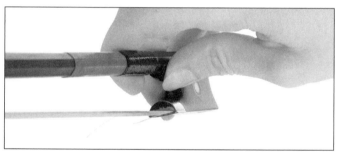

Incorrect placement of thumb

Make sure you place your middle and ring fingers together on the frog, with the pinky finger on its tip at the top of the bow. Your index finger should be positioned sideways, resting on the first knuckle, with your hand slanted slightly toward the tip of the bow.

Correct position of fingers on bow

The two types of bowings are the *up-bow* and the *down-bow*. The down-bow pulls the bow down, or toward the floor, and is represented in music by the symbol ⊓. The up-bow pushes the bow up, or toward the ceiling, and is represented by the symbol V.

Bowing the Open A String

Once you have the proper bow grip, place your bow on the open A string and practice bowing the instrument. Try to push the bow all the way up from the tip to the frog and pull all the way down from the frog to the tip. See if you can produce a good clean tone from tip to frog and from frog to tip.

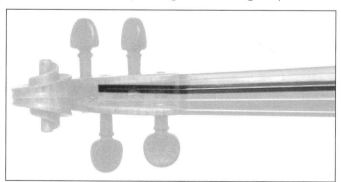

A string

Bow ready for down-bow

Bow ready for up-bow

Troubleshooting:

If you are getting a squeaky tone on your instrument:
- Make sure you aren't pressing too hard on the strings with the bow
- Make sure you are bowing on only one string at a time
- Make sure you are moving the bow as you press it into the strings
- Make sure you are bowing directly between the bridge and the fingerboard

Tuning Your Fiddle

There are several different ways to tune your fiddle. While pitch pipes, tuning forks, and in-tune pianos are all useful resources, a tuner is the most reliable way to tune your instrument.

The easiest way to learn how to tune your instrument is to sit down and place your fiddle on top of both legs with the strings facing you and the scroll pointing up. Hold the fiddle by the body with your left hand, leaving your right hand free to turn the pegs and fine tuners.

Your strings, in order from lowest to highest in pitch, are G, D, A, and E.

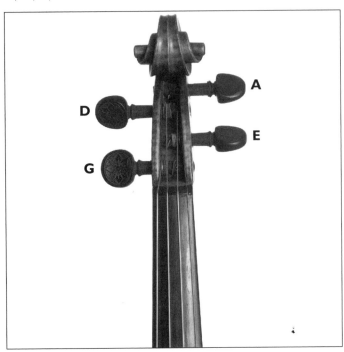

Starting with the A string, pluck the string with your thumb to see if it is close to the correct pitch. On most tuners, there is a setting that will play the note you want to tune to, and it is helpful to first listen to the tone to which you are tuning. If the A string sounds really far away from the note the tuner is playing, use the pegs up at the scroll and turn them away from you if they are too low, and toward you if they are too high. Don't turn the pegs very far or you will break a string. Turn the peg slowly, and at the same time push the string into the scroll as you tighten so it will stay in place. Repeat this with the D and G strings, and then come back to the E string.

Track 1 **Tuning to a Piano**

Track 2 **Tuning to a Fiddle**

If the string sounds close to the correct pitch, use the fine tuners (if you have them) located on your tailpiece. Turn to the right to raise the pitch, and to the left to lower the pitch.

Track 3 **Fine Tuning the Strings**

Fine tuner on fiddle

When you have finished working with the pegs and fine tuners, play an A and D together with your bow and listen if they sound in tune with each other. Repeat with the D and G strings and the A and E strings. If you hear a "wa-wa" sounding tone when the strings are played together, one or both of the strings may still be slightly out of tune and you might want to double check with the tuner one more time.

There is a "settling in" period with any new fiddle and new strings. Sometimes a string that has just been tuned will pop out of tune while you are working on the next string. Or, you may find that while playing, new strings do not hold their pitch for long. You will have to continue to re-tune them until they have settled into position.

You may also find that the tuning pegs slip out of position. Remember to push the tuning pegs into the scroll as you are turning the peg to bring the strings up to pitch, assuring that the pegs can hold their position as greater tension on the strings is created. If your tuning pegs continue to slip out of position, apply *peg drops* to each peg where it inserts into the pegheads. Most of all, HAVE PATIENCE!

The notes on the E String are: F♯, played with your index (first) finger; G♯, played with your middle (second) finger; and A, played with your ring (or third) finger.

Notes on the A String: The first finger on the A string is B, the second finger is C♯, and the third finger is D.

Notes on the D String: The first finger on the D string is E, the second finger is F♯, and the third finger is G.

Notes on the G String: The first finger on the G string is A, the second finger is B, and the third finger is C.

These are the notes you need to know to play the exercises and songs in this book.

There are more notes in between these positions, known as *chromatic* notes. The distance (or *interval*) between two notes that are right next to each other, such as between B and C or E and F, is called a *half step*. Notes that are farther apart, such as A and B or D and E, are separated by a *whole step*. A sharp (♯) raises a note by a half step, while a flat (♭) lowers a note by a half step.

The chromatic notes on the fiddle are:

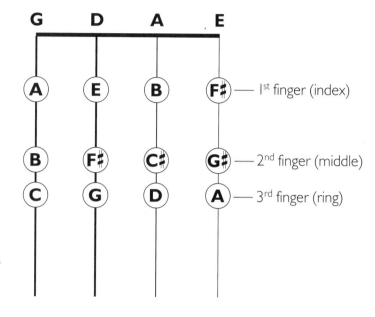

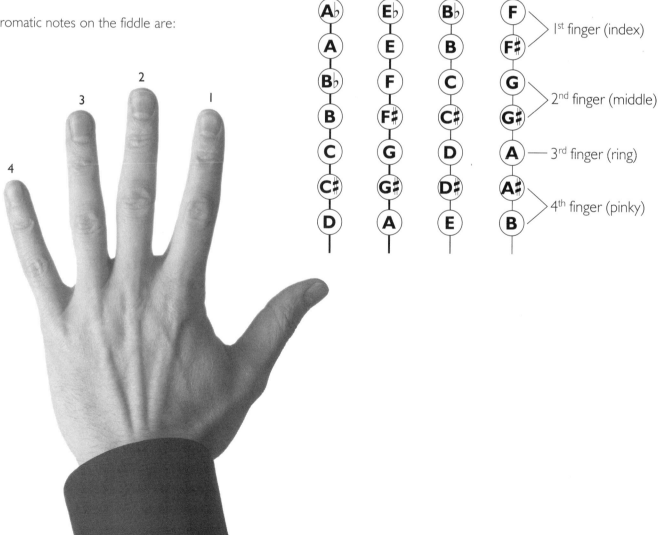

It may be helpful for you to mark where the notes lay on each string using pinstriping tape. It can be found in most music stores and is just the right thickness to stick to the fingerboard, but can also be easily removed without mess or damage to the instrument.

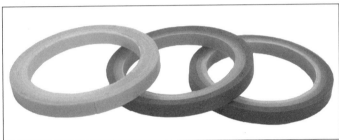

Pinstriping tape

Cut strips of the tape about two-and-a-half inches long and about a quarter of an inch wide.

With the sticky side down, slide the tape under the strings at the end of the fingerboard near the bridge.

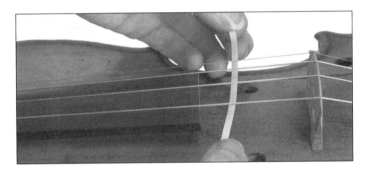

Slide tape under bridge

Slide the tape up the fingerboard to the spot where the first finger tape will be placed.

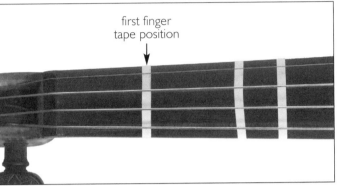

Repeat the steps until you have placed the tape at the note positions for the second and third fingers.

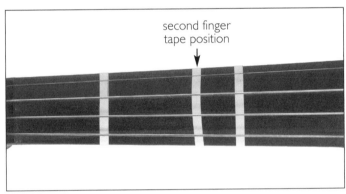

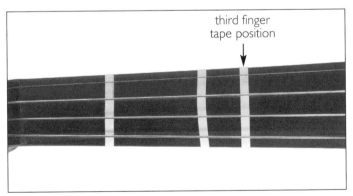

Reading Music

Reading music is really quite easy once you understand the fundamentals.

A musical note has just two properties: *pitch* and *duration*. Pitch tells you how high or low a note is and duration tells you how long the note should last.

Music is written on a *staff* (plural, *staves*), which consists of a group of five parallel lines.

A *clef* (from the French, meaning "key") is placed on the staff to identify the letter name of a set of pitches. The *G clef* (or *treble clef,* shown above) identifies the second line of the staff as the note G.

Notice that, when placed on the staff, the treble clef circles the second line, marking it as the note G.

Any of the five lines and four spaces comprising the staff can be used to represent a pitch. The lines and spaces of the staff from bottom to top indicate successively higher pitches.

Notation of Rhythm

Music has a basic *rhythm*, or *pulse,* which is created when patterns of *beats* are grouped together into larger units called *bars* or *measures* and separated by *barlines. Double* barlines show the end of a section, and *final* barlines mark the end of the tune.

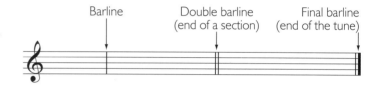

Note Values

Note value symbols represent the duration of a note. A note's *rhythmic value* is determined by its shape, stem, and flag:

Whole notes (○) equal four beats and are counted 1-2-3-4.

Half notes (♩) equal two beats, and two half notes equal one whole note.

A *quarter note (♩)* equals one beat. Two quarter notes equal a half note and four quarter notes equal a whole note.

An *eighth note (♪)* is equal to half a beat. Two eighth notes equal a quarter note, four eighth notes equal a half note, and eight eighth notes equal a whole note. Eighth notes are counted with "+" or as "ands" (1+2+3+4+), and can be grouped together by *beams.*

A *sixteenth note (♬)* is equal to a quarter of a beat. Two sixteenth notes equal one eighth note, four sixteenth notes equal a quarter note, eight sixteenth notes equal a half note, and sixteen sixteenth notes equal a whole note. Sixteenth notes are counted with "e + a" (1e+a 2e+a 3e+a 4e+a).

Basic Music Notation

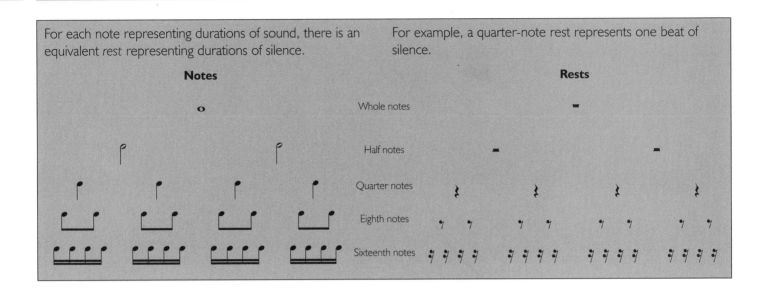

For each note representing durations of sound, there is an equivalent *rest* representing durations of silence.

For example, a quarter-note rest represents one beat of silence.

Notation of Pitch

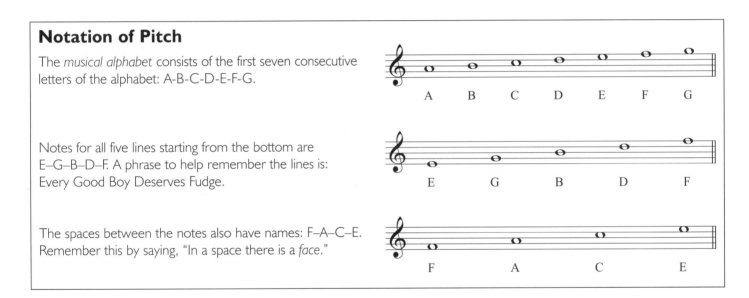

The *musical alphabet* consists of the first seven consecutive letters of the alphabet: A-B-C-D-E-F-G.

Notes for all five lines starting from the bottom are E–G–B–D–F. A phrase to help remember the lines is: Every Good Boy Deserves Fudge.

The spaces between the notes also have names: F–A–C–E. Remember this by saying, "In a space there is a *face*."

When you add the lines and spaces together, you get the musical alphabet.

Starting from the bottom line of the staff, the sequence of notes is E–F–G–A–B–C–D–E–F.

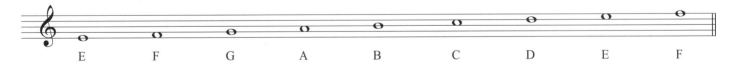

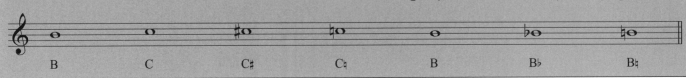

Accidentals are signs that either *raise* or *lower* a pitch by a *half step* and are placed on the staff immediately before the altered note.

- The *sharp* (♯) raises a pitch by one half step.
- The *flat* (♭) lowers a pitch by one half step.
- The *natural* (♮) cancels sharps and flats, restoring the note to its original pitch as determined by the key signature.

Ledger lines are used to extend the staff above and below its standard range of five lines.

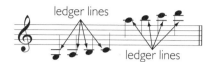

Time Signatures

The *time signature* is placed on the staff after the clef sign and consists of two numbers: the top number represents the number of beats per measure and the bottom represents the type of note that counts as one beat.

The most common time signature is $\frac{4}{4}$, or *common time*. In $\frac{4}{4}$ time, there are four quarter notes per measure.

You will also come across the following time signatures in your playing:

(two quarter notes per measure)

(three quarter notes per measure)

TIP

$\frac{4}{4}$ time is sometimes called *common time*, represented with a time signature that looks like this: **C**

Key Signatures

The *key signature* tells us what *key* the piece is in and is placed on the staff immediately after the clef sign and is notated by the use of *sharps* and *flats*.

For example, the key of D is indicated by two sharps—F♯ and C♯. This means that every F and C throughout the piece will be played as an F♯ and C♯.

The key of A has three sharps—F♯, C♯, and G♯:

The key of C has no sharps and no flats:

TIP

The key signature is repeated at the beginning of every line of music, as opposed to the time signature, which only appears at the beginning of the piece.

TIP

A sharp or flat appearing in the key signature applies to that note throughout the piece unless it is altered by the use of an accidental such as a flat, sharp, or natural.

Repeat Signs

Repeat signs indicate that the section of music within the signs should be repeated. The repeat signs appear at the beginning and end of the section to be repeated. If the repeated section includes the first measure, the repeat sign is often omitted from the beginning.

(repeat sign)   (repeat sign)

Playing on the A String

Let's practice playing half notes on the open A string.

Start with a down-bow followed by an up-bow pattern.

The numbers appearing directly above the notes indicate which finger you will use to produce that note. The "0" (zero) means that the note is played on the open string, with no fingers down.

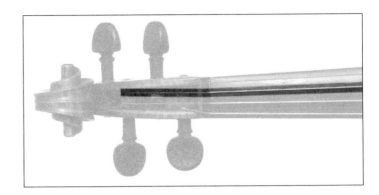

Track 4 **Half Notes on the Open A String**

Let's practice playing half notes and quarter notes together on the open A string.

Track 5 **Half Notes and Quarter Notes on the Open A String**

Now let's play half notes, quarter notes, and eighth notes together on the open A string.

Track 6 **Half Notes, Quarter Notes, and Eighth Notes on the Open A String**

Notes on the A String

Starting on the open string, play an A. Place your index finger (1) on B, then your middle finger (2) on the C♯, and finally your ring finger (3) on the D.

Track 7

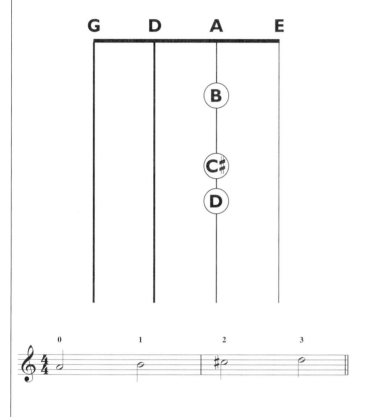

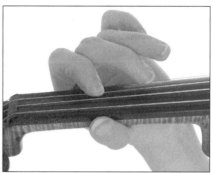

Curved finger on note B

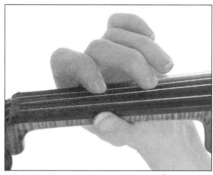

Curved finger on note C♯

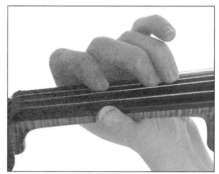

Curved finger on note D

We are going to hold each note for two beats, which is a half note in 4/4 time.

TIP	TIP
Make sure when placing fingers on the A string that you keep your fingers curved like a hook.	Play one note, stop the bow and simultaneously put down the next finger, then play.

Let's see if we can put to use what we have learned so far about notes and bowing.

On "Hot Cross Buns," start with a down-bow and use about half of the bow length for the C♯ and B, then use another quarter length of the bow for the A.

When you get to the eighth notes, remember that they are played with a faster bowstroke. Remember that the "0" means to play the open string, or no fingers down on the A string.

HOT CROSS BUNS

Track 8 Demonstration, Track 9 Backing Track

Let's try a "Run Pony, Stop Pony" rhythm, which is an eighth note followed by two sixteenth notes pattern. First try this rhythm on the open A string:

Track 10 Run Pony, Stop Pony rhythm

Run po - ny, stop po - ny, etc.

Now let's add the fingerings on the A string using the "Run Pony, Stop Pony" rhythm:

Run Pony, Stop Pony exercise

Run po - ny, stop po - ny, etc.

Here is a fiddle tune using the "Run Pony, Stop Pony" rhythm:

BOIL THE CABBAGE

Track 11 **Demonstration,** Track 12 **Backing Track**

> **TIP**
> On the song "Boil the Cabbage," keeping the "Run Pony, Stop Pony" rhythm in mind while playing each note will make it easier to play up to speed.

Let's practice switching from the open A string to the open E string:

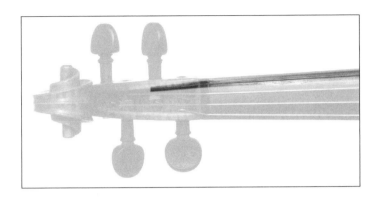

Track 13 **Switching Between the Open A and E Strings**

Notes on the E String

Now practice playing the notes on the E string. Starting on the open string, play an E. Place your index finger on F♯, then the middle finger on the G♯, and finally the third or ring finger on the A.

Track 14

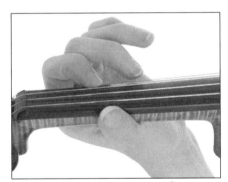

Curved finger on note F♯

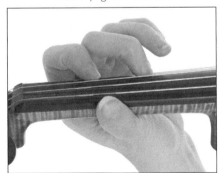

Curved finger on note G♯

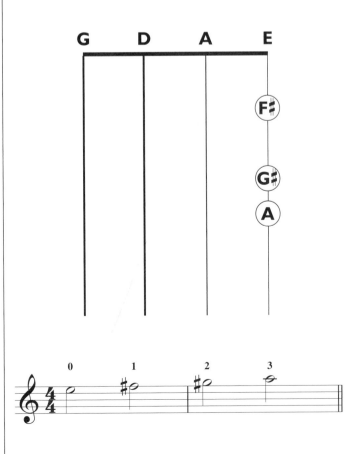

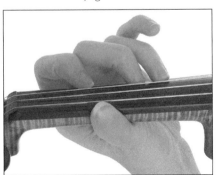

Curved finger on note A

To play the basic version of "Twinkle, Twinkle, Little Star," you will
need to use longer bowstrokes for the quarter and half notes.

TWINKLE, TWINKLE, LITTLE STAR
(BASIC VERSION)

Track 15 **Demonstration, Track 16** **Backing Track**

Now we are ready to try the "Chugga Chugga, Stop Stop" rhythm on the open strings:

Track 17 **Chugga Chugga, Stop Stop rhythm**

Chug - ga chug - ga, stop stop, etc.

Remember

If you are getting a squeaky tone on your instrument:
- Make sure you aren't pressing too hard on the strings with the bow
- Make sure the bow is placed directly between the bridge and the fingerboard

- Make sure you are playing on only one string at a time
- Make sure you are moving the bow at the same time as you are pressing into the bow

---

TIP

Always remember to stop the bow between each rhythm to make a clean sound. Before crossing between two strings, it is also helpful to make sure you have stopped the bow completely before going on to the next string.

Once you have mastered "Twinkle, Twinkle, Little Star" in its
basic version, try this variation using the "Chugga Chugga,
Stop Stop" rhythm.

TWINKLE, TWINKLE, LITTLE STAR
(CHUGGA CHUGGA VARIATION)

Track 18 **Demonstration,** Track 19 **Backing Track**

Chug-ga chug-ga, stop stop, chug-ga chug-ga, stop stop, *etc.*

TIP
Remember to stop your bow in between each note for a clean tone.

The duration of a note can be altered with the addition of a *dot* placed immediately after the note, which increases its value by one half.

Now try the following exercise that uses the pattern of a dotted quarter note followed by an eighth note on the open A string. Remember that the dotted quarter gets one and a half beats and the eighth note gets half a beat.

Track 20 **Dotted Exercise #1**

Now let's move on and add some of the notes on the A string:

Track 21 **Dotted Exercise #2**

Track 22 **Dotted Exercise #3**

This last exercise using dotted rhythms will prepare us for a fiddle tune called "Liza Jane":

Track 23 **Dotted Exercise #4**

Dotted Rhythms

Now try this popular fiddle tune:

LIZA JANE

Track 24 **Demonstration,** Track 25 **Backing Track**

Now let's transfer all of the exercises that we have just learned over to the D string.

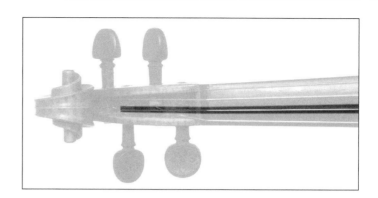

Practice playing on the open D string:

Notes on the D string

Now practice playing the notes on the D string. Starting on the open string, play a D. Place your index finger on E, then your middle finger on the F♯, and finally your third (ring) finger on the G.

Track 26

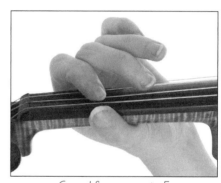

Curved finger on note E

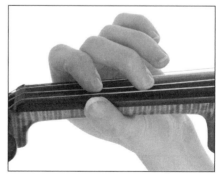

Curved finger on note F♯

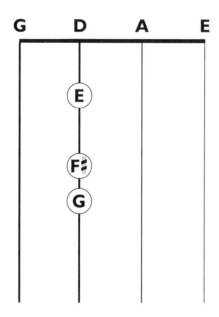

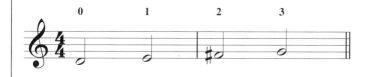

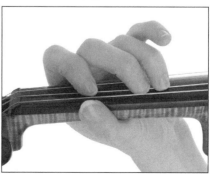

Curved finger on note G

Playing on the D String

Now let's try the notes on the D string starting on the open D:

Track 27 Notes on the D String Exercise

Let's try some sixteenth-note rhythms on the open D string:

Track 28 Sixteenth Notes on the D String

Now try the different rhythm patterns you've learned on the D string, starting with the "Run Pony, Stop Pony" rhythm:

Let's try the "Chugga Chugga, Stop Stop" rhythm:

The Major Scale

Remember that the distance between all natural notes is a *whole step*, except in two instances: between B and C, and E and F, there is only the difference of a *half step*.

A *scale* is a sequence of seven notes in a specific whole- and half-step pattern.

The *major* scale pattern is as follows:

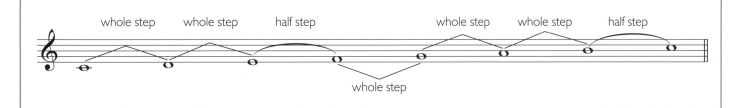

Try the D major scale scale using the dotted rhythm pattern:

Track 29 **D String Exercise #2**

Let's try a tune using the D string.

OH, SUSANNA

Track 30 **Demonstration,** Track 31 **Backing Track**

TIP
When a piece of music does not begin on the first beat of the measure, the notes that occur before the downbeat are called the *anacrusis*, sometimes referred to as an *upbeat* or *pick-up*.

We have finally arrived at the G string, the lowest string on the fiddle. Let's combine what we have learned on the A, D, and E strings.

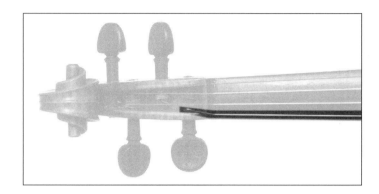

Practice half notes on the open G string:

Notes on the G String

Now practice playing the notes on the G string. Starting on the open string, play a G. Place your index finger on the A, then your middle finger on the B, and finally your third (ring) finger on the C.

Track 32

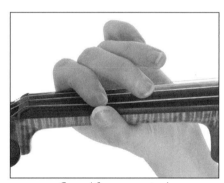

Curved finger on note A

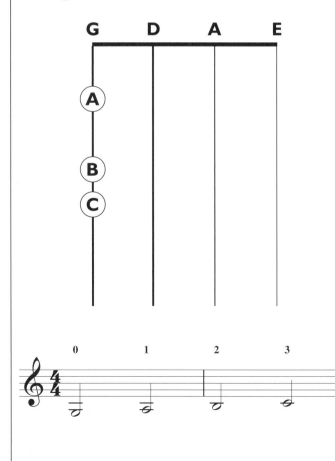

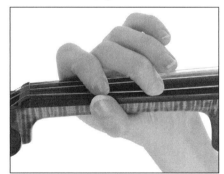

Curved finger on note B

Curved finger on note C

Start by practicing the notes on the G string in half-note and quarter-note patterns.

Track 33 **Notes on the G string exercise**

Now let's practice starting on the G string and playing a scale using all four strings:

Track 34 **G Major Scale in Quarter Notes**

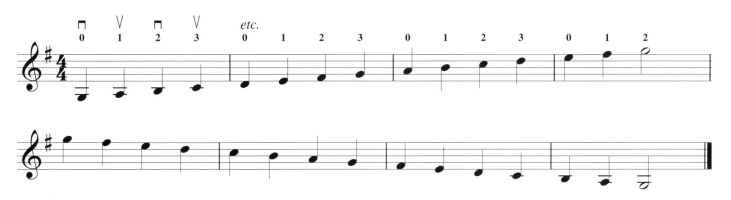

Try this same scale using eighth notes:

Track 35 **G Major Scale in Eighth Notes**

Now play this same scale using sixteenth notes:

Track 36 **G Major Scale in Sixteenth Notes**

Playing on the G String

Let's try and play a very old fiddle tune called
"Dem Golden Slippers":

DEM GOLDEN SLIPPERS

Track 37 **Demonstration,** Track 38 **Backing Track**

There are many different ways to *kickoff*, or introduce, fiddle tunes. The most common kickoff for a bluegrass-type fiddle tune is called "Four Potatoes Among Fiddlers" and uses two strings played at once, known as a *double stop*.

When playing double stops, press into the open strings evenly so they sound at an equal volume. First practice double stops in a slow, whole- or half-note pattern to get a feel for how the bow should be weighted on the strings. Then try the following kickoffs.

If the fiddle tune is in the key of A, you will play the kickoff on the open A and E strings.

Track 39 **Kickoff in A**

If the fiddle tune is in the key of D, you will play on the open D and A strings.

Track 40 **Kickoff in D**

> **TIP**
> Double stops are created when two adjacent strings are played at the same time. When you are playing double stops, press into the open strings evenly so that both notes sound at an equal volume.

There are also many different endings that can be tagged onto a fiddle tune to conclude it.

These are called *tag endings*. First try these tag endings in the key of A:

Track 41 **Tag Ending in A #1**

Track 42 **Tag Ending in A #2**

Track 43 **Tag Ending in A #3**

Track 44 **Tag Ending in A #4**

Now try these tag endings in the key of D:

Track 45 **Tag Ending in D #1**

Track 46 **Tag Ending in D #2**

Track 47 **Tag Ending in D #3**

Track 48 **Tag Ending in D #4**

TIP

On the more difficult tag endings, first practice the notes slowly, stopping between each bowstroke to maintain a clean sound.

These last tunes incorporate all that you have learned in this book. "Devil's Dream" and "Old Joe Clark" are two of the oldest and most popular fiddle tunes. These tunes also incorporate some difficult bowing techniques and fingerings.

On "Devil's Dream," first listen to Track 49 on the CD and then take one line at a time until you can play it through without any mistakes.

DEVIL'S DREAM

Track 49 **Demonstration, Track** 50 **Backing Track**

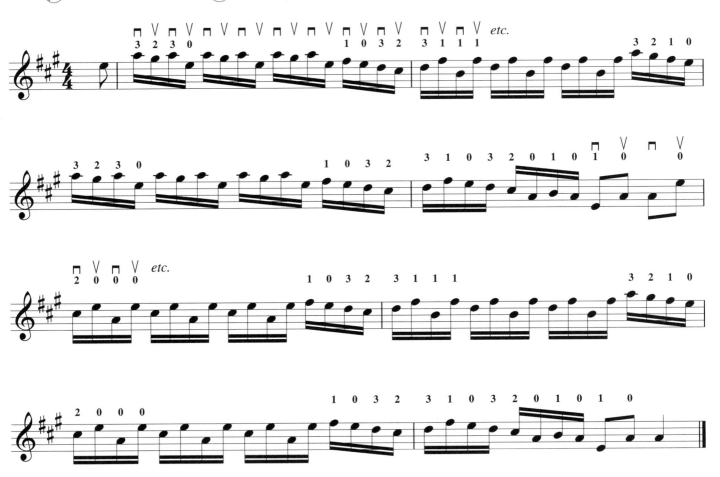

OLD JOE CLARK

Track 51 **Demonstration, Track** 52 **Backing Track**

CAMPTOWN RACES

Track 53 **Demonstration**, Track 54 **Backing Track**

CRIPPLE CREEK

Track 55 **Demonstration**, Track 56 **Backing Track**

Congratulations!

I hope that you have enjoyed learning the basics of fiddling and that you will feel inspired to continue learning the fiddle. If you made it through the book successfully and can play along with the CD, you should be able to move on to learn some more difficult tunes and maybe even get together and jam with other beginners. Or, get together with other more advanced fiddlers and musicians and try to play along. Find fiddle contests, jam sessions, and bluegrass festivals in your area and watch other fiddlers perform live.

LISTEN, LISTEN, LISTEN! Listen to all of the fiddle music you can get your hands on. Some of my favorite bluegrass fiddlers who were most influential to me include, Benny Martin, Paul Warren, Scotty Stoneman, Bobby Hicks, Stuart Duncan, Craig Duncan, Byron Berline, Chubby Wise, Mark O'Connor, Diane Sprouse, Tommy Jackson, Roger Smith, and Ed Cosner.

Discography

Kenny Baker
Master Fiddler (County 2705)

Kenny Baker and Bobby Hicks
Darkness on the Delta (County 2733)

Bluegrass Album Band
Bluegrass Album, Vol. 1 (Rounder CD-0140)
Bluegrass Album, Vol. 2 (Rounder CD-0164)
Bluegrass Album, Vol. 3: California Connection
  (Rounder CD-0180)
Bluegrass Album, Vol. 4 (Rounder CD-0210)
Bluegrass Album, Vol. 5: Sweet Sunny South
  (Rounder CD-0240)

Stuart Duncan
Stuart Duncan (Rounder 263)

Lester Flatt & Earl Scruggs
The Complete Mercury Sessions (Mercury 314-512644-2)
Flatt and Scruggs, 1959-1963 (Bear Family Records
  [BCD] 15559)
Flatt and Scruggs, 1964-1969 (Bear Family Records
  [BCD] 1587)
'Tis Sweet To Be Remembered: The Essential Flatt and Scruggs
  (Columbia/Legacy 64877)

Bill Monroe & His Bluegrass Boys
Bluegrass Instrumentals (Decca D-74601)
The High Lonesome Sound of Bill Monroe (D-74780)

Mark O'Connor
Heroes (Warner Bros. 45257-2)
The New Nashville Cats (Warner Bros. 2-26509)
Soppin' the Gravy (Rounder CD-0137)

Ricky Skaggs
Big Mon: The Songs of Bill Monroe (Skaggs Family 1002)

Ricky Skaggs and Kentucky Thunder
Instrumentals (Skaggs Family 01007)

Tony Rice
Manzanita (Rounder CD-0092)

Scotty Stoneman
Fiddle and Banjo Blue Grass (Arion 64143)
Live in L.A. (Rural Rhythm 1017)

Originally from Illinois, Gail Rudisill-Johnson now makes her home near Nashville, Tennessee. She began classical violin lessons at the age of 5, and by the age of 14 was competing in regional and state competitions, winning the Illinois State Fiddle Competition and placing in the top two in many others. Over the next few years, she performed on the bluegrass circuit, as well as attended the Belmont University School of Music in Nashville. Johnson went on to obtain a bachelor's degree in music with an emphasis in violin performance. After graduation, she started performing at the Grand Ole Opry with "Whispering" Bill Anderson and remained with his band for eight years. Currently an active teacher, Johnson also plays violin/fiddle on various recording sessions, and develops and promotes the annual Wabash River Music Camp and Festival in Southern Illinois.

Also from the Music Sales
Fiddle Collection

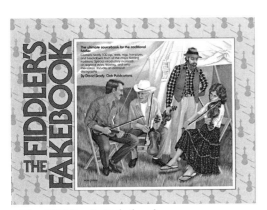

The Fiddler's Fakebook
By David Brody
Contains nearly 500 jigs, reels, rags, and hornpipes from all the major fiddling traditions. Special introductory materials on regional styles, bowing, and ornamentation. Includes an extensive discography.
OK63925
ISBN 0.8256.0238.6
ISBN-13: 978.0.8256.0238.2
UPC 7.52187.63925.1

The Fiddle Book
By Marion Thede
The most comprehensive collection of traditional fiddle tunes ever compiled. Contains over 150 tunes, familiar and obscure, with lyrics. Transcribed from the playing of country fiddlers.
OK61853
ISBN 0.8256.0145.2
ISBN-13: 978.0.8256.0145.3
UPC 7.52187.61853.9

Bluegrass Fiddle Styles
By Stacy Phillips and Kenny Kosek
The most complete bluegrass fiddle book ever published. Authentic transcriptions of bluegrass breaks in the styles of 25 major players, including Eck Robertson, Chubby Wise, Vassar Clements, and Kenny Baker.
OK63487
ISBN 0.8256.0185.1
ISBN-13: 978.0.8256.0185.9
UPC 7.52187.63487.4

50 Fiddle Solos
By Seane Keane
Seane Keane, popular fiddler of the Chieftains, has selected, arranged, and recorded 50 superb jigs, reels, and hornpipes. With accompanying CD. Featuring other members of the Chieftains.
AM970497
ISBN 0.7119.8864.1
ISBN-13: 978.0.7119.8864.4
UPC 7.52187.97049.1

Fiddle Case Tunebook: British Isles
By Stacy Phillips
Music for 50 fiddle tunes from Ireland, England, Scotland, and Wales. This book also includes a discography and tips on authentic techniques and interpretation. Conveniently sized at 4.5 by 12 inches.
AM71317
ISBN 0.8256.2545.9
ISBN-13: 978.0.8256.2545.9
UPC 7.52187.71317.3

Fiddle Case Tunebook: Old-Time Southern
By Stacy Phillips
Here are 50 fiddle tunes from the old-time repertoire of the American South, arranged with bowings and phrasings. Complete with notation, tips on interpretation, and a discography.
AM71309
ISBN 0.8256.2544.0
ISBN-13: 978.0.8256.2544.2
UPC 7.52187.11124.5

Oak Publications
A part of *The **Music Sales** Group*

ABSOLUTE BEGINNERS
Fiddle

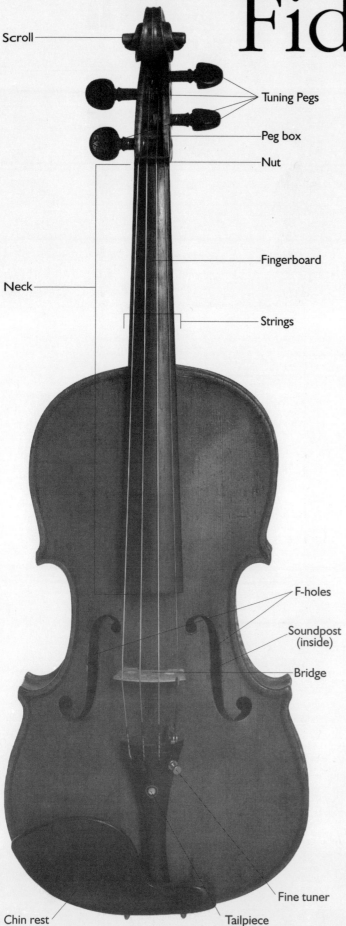

Scroll

Tuning Pegs

Peg box

Nut

Fingerboard

Neck

Strings

F-holes

Soundpost
(inside)

Bridge

Fine tuner

Chin rest

Tailpiece

Parts of the Fiddle

The *scroll* is located at the top of the fiddle and is often decorative.

The *tuning pegs* are used to adjust the tuning of the fiddle by tightening or loosening the strings, and are inserted into the *peg box*.

The fiddle has four *strings*: G, D, A, and E.

The *fingerboard* runs down the length of the *neck* and is where the player presses the strings down to play notes.

The *f-holes* (so-called because they are shaped like the cursive letter "f") allow for more sound to resonant from the instrument.

The *bridge* is held in place by and supports the tension of the strings stretched over the body of the fiddle and transmits the vibrations of the strings throughout the body of the instrument.

The *soundpost* is located under bridge, inside the fiddle, and supports the body of the instrument as well as helps amplify the sound of the instrument.

The *fine tuners* are used for making subtle adjustments to the tuning that do not require the loosening or tightening of the string at the tuning peg.

The *tailpiece* and *nut* hold and support the strings across the length of the instrument.

The *chin rest* helps the fiddler keep the instrument in place under the chin, keeping the fingering (left) hand free from having to support the instrument.

Taking Care of Your Fiddle

Fiddles are fragile, so be sure to take good care of your instrument:

1. Don't bump the fiddle into anything or drop it at any time.
2. Try not to expose the instrument to extreme heat or cold. At the very least, the strings will pop out of tune.
3. Make sure to wipe off the body of the fiddle and the fiddle strings after every time you play.

Notes on the Fiddle

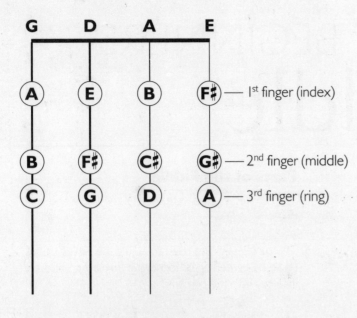

1st finger (index)

2nd finger (middle)

3rd finger (ring)

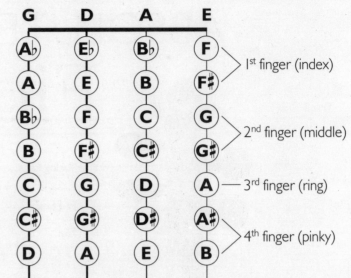

1st finger (index)

2nd finger (middle)

3rd finger (ring)

4th finger (pinky)

Notes on the G String

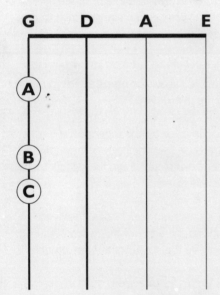

Notes on the D String

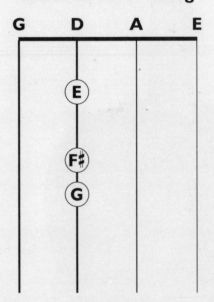

Notes on the A String

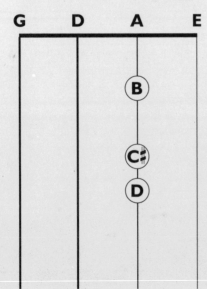

Notes on the E String

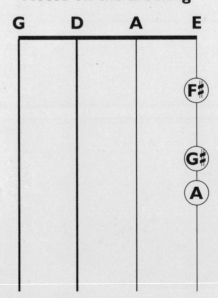

Pull-OutChart